So, you think you've got problems?

Rosalind Birkett

Egon Publishers Ltd
618 Leeds Road, Outwood, Wakefield, WF1 2LT

First Published in 1993
Reprinted in 1995
Third Impression 1999
Fourth Impression 2005
Fifth Impression 2009
Second Edition 2011

Egon Publishers Ltd
618 Leeds Road, Outwood
Wakefield, West Yorkshire, WF1 2LT

Copyright (c) Rosalind Birkett

ISBN: 978 1907656 01 9

So, you think you've got problems?

For Nejat

This is a book for you.

Lots and lots of
books have been
written for teachers,
and your Mums
and Dads,
so I thought it
was high time
you had one all
to yourselves.

Lots and lots and lots of people all over the world have had problems with learning to read, write, spell, write stories and do sums.

It has happened for a long, long time. These people were often told that they were stupid or lazy.

People have the same problems today, but now lots and lots of people understand, and can show them that they are not stupid or lazy, and that they can do it!

All they need is a little bit of help to learn in a different way, and they can do very well if they are just shown how.

Lots and lots and lots of people find it very difficult to copy from the board.

They look up to start at the beginning, and then look down to see where they should write on their page.

When they look up again they have lost their place, so they have to find it again. This can be very tricky.

They may find they have gone back to the wrong line, and then they get in a terrible muddle. It can be very tiring and very slow.

Sometimes their teachers tell them to hurry up and not to be lazy.

The trouble is that they are not being lazy. They are working very hard and it makes them cross or sad.

Lots and lots and lots of people find it very hard to learn to read.

Sometimes, when they see a word they cannot remember it for very long.

When they see that word again they have forgotten what it was.

This is because a small part of their memory isn't working quite as well as the rest of their memory (which is working very well indeed).

It's nobody's fault, it's just the way it is.

Lots and lots and lots of people get their letters back to front and write 'd' for 'b', and 'p' for 'q'.

It is very confusing: 't' for 'f', 'u' for 'n' all round the wrong way. It is because they find it hard to see the difference, and hard to remember which way they go.

Lots and lots and lots of people write backwards. That's very clever, not everyone can do that, but it does get muddling.

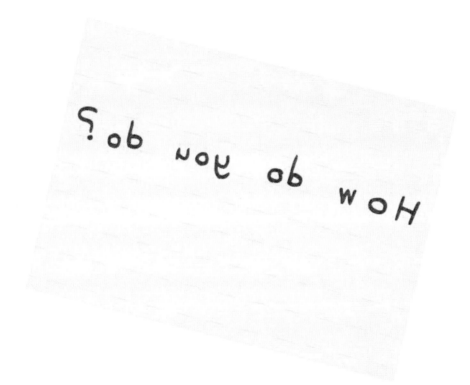

Maybe they hear it backwards too.

Lots and lots and lots of people can do sums very well but often get them wrong because they put 12 for 21 and UT instead of TU.

It's not their fault; it's just that things get rather jumbled sometimes.

Lots and lots and lots of people find it very hard to remember all the things that they have been asked to do.

Then they might get into trouble for not listening. Not fair is it?

Lots and lots and lots of people find it hard to think of anything to write for a story. When they do, the end may come before the beginning.

They may have tried very hard, but what a mix and muddle it is!

Lots and lots and lots of people find spelling almost impossible to learn. However hard they try, they always seem to get them wrong.

Do you ever feel like that?

Well, how do we sort out these problems?

First of all, it is a good idea to go with your Mum and Dad to see someone who really understands your problems.

You will play a few games, and answer a few questions – some of the things you will find easy and some of the things you will find more difficult.

That's O.K. That's how it should be.

When you have finished, your Mum and Dad may go in and have a chat to find out the best way to help you.

After that you may have a 'special' lesson each week with a 'special' teacher.

You will be able to tell her about all the things that worry you – she will understand your particular problems.

Soon you will see that you are much better at some things than most people, and that the bits that were difficult are not quite so difficult anymore.

You will probably get your 'b's' and 'd's' mixed up sometimes, but not nearly as often as before. Reading and writing will be easier too.

You will stop worrying so much because you know that someone understands. Instead of getting things wrong, you will be getting them right.

There is nothing wrong with you. All you need is a different way to learn – and you will learn, very well.

Just you wait and see.